My Time With The Most High

Deuteronomy Means "Do The Right Thing!"

Tara La Sean

The Lord's Prayer

Our Father (Ahayah) which art in Heaven, Hallowed be thy name. Thy kingdom come, Thy will be done in earth, as it is in Heaven. Give us this day our daily bread. And forgive us our debts as we forgive our debtors. And lead us not into temptation, but deliver us from evil: For thine is the kingdom, and the power, and the glory, forever.

Ahayah Bahasham Yashaya Wa Rawach

(In the name of the Father, the Son and the Holy Spirit)

Amen

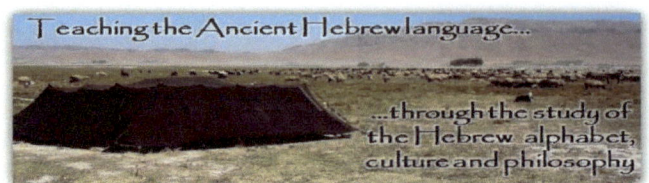

GET YOUR HEBREW ON!!

As we learn more about the laws, statutes, commands and culture of the Ancient Israelites, it is just as important to learn some of the language they spoke. By learning some of the words and phrases in their language of Ancient Phonetic Hebrew we can connect even more to our forefathers and to Ahayah! See if you can learn the words below and use them in a sentence (Advanced students should find a scripture containing these words and write it out, substituting the English word for the Hebrew word). Practice saying them often!

1. *Mayim=* Water.

2. *Rawach=* Spirit.

3. *Ben=* Son.

4. *Bath=* Daughter.

5. *Torah=* Law

What Can You Remember?

Before diving into the fifth book of the Bible, Deuteronomy, let's do a quick review of what we have covered so far in the previous books of this series. Challenge yourself to remember as much as you can before you look up the answer**s.**

Genesis: Name three patriarchs from this book and give two points about them.
_____
_____
_____
_____
_____

Exodus: Give two examples of the wicked things Pharaoh did to the Israelites.
_____
_____
_____
_____

Leviticus: Name the four types of laws and give an example of each.
_____
_____
_____
_____
_____
_____
_____

Numbers: What reports were given of Canaan by the spies?
_____
_____
_____
_____
_____

It's A BIG Job!

According to Deuteronomy chapter one, Moses chose men to be leaders over various groups of Israelites. Explain what type of men he chose, why he had to choose them and what their duties would be.

BEE Creative! Read Deuteronomy 4:7 and give examples of what *you* call upon Ahayah for. Draw pictures, write poems or make up a story about the things TMH has done for you!

Name: _____

Walking Into The Promises! Complete the crossword below

Created with TheTeachersCorner.net Crossword Puzzle Generator

Across
2. What kind of God is TMH that He doesn't want us to worship other gods?
3. Who did Ahayah speak face-to-face with?
6. Who would the Children of Israel be scattered among?
8. Area by the bank of Arnon.
9. What land was Sihon king of?
10. What land was Og the king of?

Down
1. Which tribes inhabited land from Gilead to Arnon? (3 words)
4. Besides Deut. 5, what other book of the Bible has the 10 commandments?
5. What did TMH desire Israel to have to fear Him and keep His commandments?
7. Where did Ahayah make the covenant with Israel?

MANY ABOMINATIONS!

The Book of Deuteronomy makes several references to things Ahayah considers to be abominations. Read the following passages and write out what the abomination is and why the act described is detestable to TMH.

Deut. 7:25
_____
_____
_____
_____
_____
_____

Deut. 13:12-15
_____
_____
_____
_____
_____
_____
_____

Deut. 18:9-12
_____
_____
_____
_____
_____

Don't Be Led Astray!

Like us, our forefathers were sometimes approached by friends, family members and highly respected people who try to lead us away from Ahayah. Read chapter 13 carefully and discuss how these people would try to trick the children of Israel in the past and compare it to how they are still deceiving people today (This activity can be done by a group as well. See appendix for suggestions).

Name: _____

What's on the Menu? Deut. Ch. 14

Use the KJV Bible to help complete the crossword below.

Across

2. What food category of birds are owls, kites and hawks?
5. If an animal's hoof is _____, he might be clean.
9. The Children of Israel must not eat any _____ thing.
10. If an animal dies of itself, who can you sell the meat to?

Down

1. What two traits must seafood have to be clean? (3 words)
3. The ____ tribe has no inheritance?
4. If an animal chews this, it might be clean.
6. What can't you make between your eyes?
7. What type of Holy people did TMH chose Israel to be?
8. After how many years were we to bring tithes in the Old Testament?

ALL YE, ALL YE, OUTS IN FREE!!

Hide-and-go-seek is my all-time favorite game! Finding the best hiding places and trying to outrun the person who is "it" if you are discovered are parts of the fun of course, but the very best part is when they yell "All ye, All ye, Outs in free!" This was the signal that it was safe to come out of hiding and return to "home base" without penalty. Because we had been disobedient to Ahayah, He "hid" His face from us and we were made to suffer in Egypt. But once He brought us out of bondage, He gave us His law to bring us back to his love and protection. Review the Book of Deuteronomy chapters 1-16 and tell how following the law brings us back to TMH. Be sure to give examples of the law (This is an advanced lesson and can be modified. See appendix).

Sweet 16

See if you can find the words hidden in the puzzle from Deuteronomy Ch. 16 KJV.

```
M V Y Z X X N F A H S A C R I F I C E L
R U M J W D E S S E L B H N F Z T U B B
H K R U F Z I J N N T S N Q V Y W N G P
S C S X E K R L N Q U F H H U H D L P K
S K X Z B V V E V O R G G H N K Z E C N
W H A H T N E V E S V M I T A J Q A J J
D U N H M N D Q R H Y N C S M W P V E K
Q E L K C I S A T M B C N U D K X E S G
A P Y U P E C N A T I R E H N I U N O G
K F G S S E L R E H T A F T O A F E L U
O M D S B O P E I X T X B A B S R D E N
H G U T O N I Y L L S M E P N R E C M H
K A T R B Q G L S C I U W O C K M N N I
C D V A S P A P N N A B Z V P A E E S P
S P W N E L M S L O E N R D T W M U A Y
O T J G R K S Q W G S E R F J U B I B R
V P R E V O S S A P Z A E E M M E H I Z
T N Y R E J J M L F Y A E B B H R Q B U
V S S M I K I R H R S U L S L A X B P O
N Q E P W I D O W T J A D T A T T H K M
```

SACRIFICE	ABIB	SOLEMN
GROVE	INHERITANCE	TABERNACLE
UNLEAVENED	IMAGE	OBSERVE
REMEMBER	BONDMAN	SEASON
SEVENTH	FATHERLESS	SICKLE
WIDOW	STRANGER	FEAST
BLESSED	PASSOVER	

$$TITHING: *REWIND/ FAST FORWARD*

There are many people who question the practice of tithing. The idea of giving 10% of everything you earn to a church or spiritual teacher is uncomfortable for some. Let's examine the scriptures to learn why tithing was started and if it is a practice we should still follow.

⏪ Tithing was practiced long before TMH gave Moses the law. How does Gen. 14:17-20 prove this? Who gave tithes? Who were the tithes given to?

_____
_____
_____
_____

⏸ Deuteronomy 14:20 clearly states in the law that a tithe of all our increase must be given each year. Who, according to verses 28-29 are the tithes for?

_____
_____
_____
_____

⏩ Malachi 3:8-12 beautifully describes the "what's in it for me" where tithes are concerned. What does this passage say about not giving a tithe as well as what will happen if you do?

_____
_____
_____
_____

⏭ Let's jump further ahead for an *advanced question*. Tithing is mentioned several times in the New Testament. Find one scripture that shows tithing was still important during/ after Yashaya's time.

_____
_____
_____
_____

HARSH PUNISHMENT

Have you ever gotten in trouble at home or at school and thought the punishment you received was too harsh for what you did? As children, we all feel that way sometimes but as we get older we begin to understand that the punishment was given out of our parents' love for us. We learn that they want us to stay safe and protected so they are hard on us. Ahayah is the same way. Read Deut. 17 and discuss why the punishments He gave for certain wicked deeds were so severe.

Ahayah Fights My Battles!!

Use Deut.20 in the KJV and the words in the list below to complete the sentences.

> TRIBUTARIES   CHARIOTS   BATTLE   DESTROY   BESIEGE   OFFICERS
>
> TREMBLE   BETROTHED   ABOMINATIONS   BULWARKS

1. "And what man hath _____ a wife…"
2. "And thou shalt build _____ against the city that maketh war with thee. Until it be subdued.
3. "And if it will make no peace with thee, but will make war against thee, then thou shalt _____ it. "
4. "That they teach you not to do after their _____."
5. "Let not your hearts faint, fear not, and do not _____."
6. Thou shalt not _____ the trees thereof by forcing an axe against them."
7. "When ye are come nigh unto the _____ the priests shall approach."
8. "When thou goest out to battle against thine enemies and you see horses and _____ be not afraid."
9. "All the people that is found therein shall be _____ , unto thee, and they shall serve thee.
10. "And the _____ shall speak unto the people saying…"

BETTER OBEY YOUR PARENTS!

Read Deut. 21:18-21 and explain what happens when children don't obey their parents. Remember, Ahayah is also our parent!

UN-HOLY ABOMINATIONS, BATMAN!

Match the following scriptures to the pictures below to show your understanding of what Ahayah says are abominations (D. = Deut. and L.= Lev.).

D. 15:23   L. 20:13   D.14:10   D. 22:5   D. 17:1   D. 7:25   D. 14:3   D. 24:4   D. 18:10

A

B

C

_____   _____   _____

D

E

F

_____   _____   _____

G

H

I

_____   _____   _____

The 12 Tribes of Israel
Genesis 49

Reuben
Abor of Australia/ Sem Indians

Simeon
Dominicans

Levi
Haitians

Judah
African Americans

Zebulon
Panamanians

Ephraim
Puerto Ricans

Mannaseh
Cubans

Naphtali
Hawaiians/Pac Islanders

Gad
North Amer Indians

Asher
South & Central Americans

Issachar
Mexicans

Benjamin
Jamaicans/ W Indies

WHERE IN THE WORLD?

Using the 12 Tribes chart from the previous page, find the area that each tribe settled into and mark it with the <u>first letter</u> of the tribe's name. Some tribes were in more than one area so you can mark that as well! Which tribe is NOT shown on this map (Advanced question)?

This Happened to Who??

Both the Bible and world history points to certain people being the true children of Israel. How can you use Deuteronomy chapter 28 to prove this? (Advanced students are encouraged to include Genesis 49, the 12 Tribes Sign and both secular and biblical history in their answers.)

_____
_____
_____
_____
_____
_____
_____
_____
_____
_____
_____
_____
_____
_____
_____
_____
_____
_____
_____
_____
_____
_____
_____
_____
_____
_____
_____

PROMISES, PROMISES!

Ahayah promised the Children of Israel many wonderful things if they would obey His laws, statutes and commands! Read Deuteronomy 28:1-14 and give three examples of how Israel would be blessed for obeying Ahayah. Be sure to explain what the blessing is and which verse you are using!

Promise One

Promise Two

Promise Three

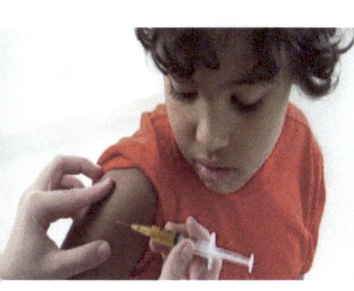

And the Curses…

Read Deuteronomy 28:15-45 and discuss how the children of Israel (from any tribe) fit three of these curses for their disobedience. Be sure to give the verse you are discussing.

Curse One

Curse Two

Curse Three

Blessed or Cursed?
Find the words below from the Book of Deuteronomy KJV.

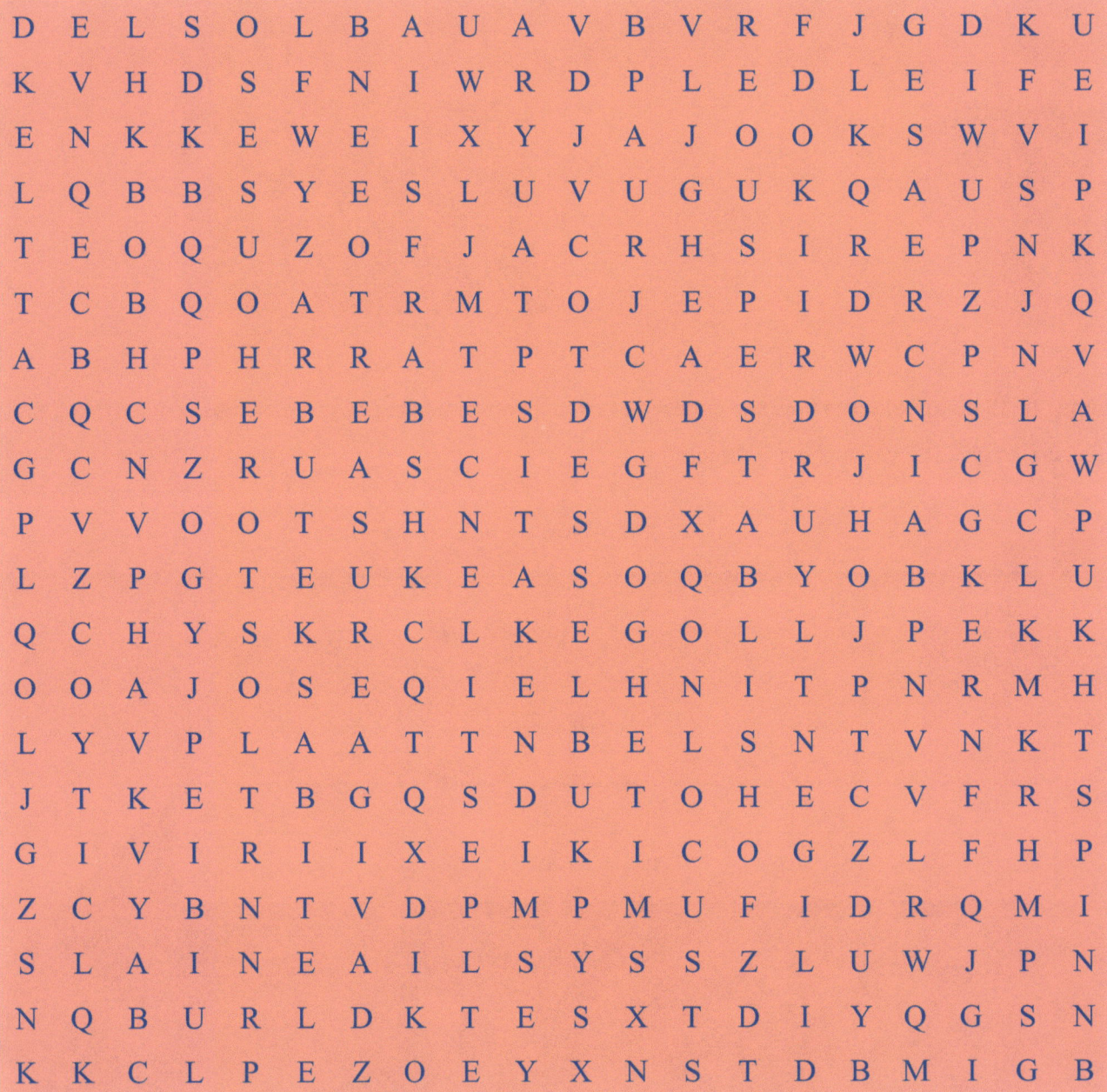

ESTABLISH	SLAIN	HEAD
CITY	PERISH	FRUIT
FIELD	PESTILENCE	BASKET
KINE	GROPE	PLENTEOUS
STOREHOUSE	CATTLE	TAKEN
BLESSED	SMITE	TREASURE
LOCUSTS	DILIGENTLY	CAPTIVITY
DESTROYED	INCREASE	OVERTAKE

Sabbath Day Law Quest

Read the following passages carefully and choose the correct scripture in the KJV bible where it is found.

1. And he shall wave the sheaf before the Lord, to be accepted for you: on the morrow after the sabbath the priest shall wave it.
   - Deut. 10:6
   - Lev. 19:3
   - Ex. 25:1
   - Lev. 23:11

2. Ye shall kindle no fire throughout your habitations upon the sabbath day.
   - Lev. 9:5
   - Ex. 35:3
   - Deut. 11:2
   - Gen. 6:8

3. Every sabbath he shall set it in order before the Lord continually, being taken from the children of Israel by an everlasting covenant.
   - Lev. 25:6
   - Ex. 16:23
   - Lev. 24:8
   - Deut. 6:4

4. Keep the sabbath day to sanctify it, as the Lord thy God hath commanded thee.
   - Deut. 5:12
   - Num. 3:3
   - Gen. 8:1
   - Deut. 5:14

5. Ye shall keep my sabbaths, and reverence my sanctuary: I am the Lord.
   - Deut. 7:10
   - Lev. 26:2
   - Num. 5:5
   - Lev. 28:1

6. And remember that thou wast a servant in the land of Egypt, and that the Lord thy God brought thee out thence through a mighty hand and by a stretched out arm: therefore the Lord thy God commanded thee to keep the sabbath day.
   - Lev. 26:43
   - Num. 28:9
   - Deut. 5:15
   - Lev. 25:6

Deuteronomy 30:15-20 begins with: "See, I have set before thee this day life and good, and death and evil." Think back over the book of Deuteronomy and tell what you think this verse meant to our ancestors who were given the law, as well as what it means for Israelites today.

WRAP-UP

As Deuteronomy is the fifth and final book of the Law, it seems right to end this book a bit differently from the others. We have spent a good deal of time learning about the Law of Ahayah as it was given to Moses. We have also learned how important it is to keep the civil, ceremonial, dietary and moral laws, statutes and commands of TMH and His Son Yashaya. With that said, for this wrap-up lesson I challenge you to reflect on these laws and think about the areas you need to work on personally. Then, choose one thing you struggle with most (obeying your parents, telling the truth, forgiving others, etc.) and make a commitment to TMH to do better in that area.

You do not have to write out your plan formally, but I encourage you to keep a journal or notebook to track your progress. This should be an agreement between you and Ahayah that you take **_very seriously_**. As you read the Bible, write down scriptures you come across to help you do better.

Fasting is also a great way to strengthen ourselves and to show TMH we are serious about wanting to be closer to Him. Remember, fasting is not always from food; you can fast from a lot of things such as video games, T.V., dessert or playing with your favorite toy (I sometimes fast from my cell phone and playing Angry Birds!). It's about being willing to sacrifice what we like for TMH. And don't forget to pray! Some habits are hard to break, but He will help us if we ask Him in faith and in sincerity.

ALL PRAISES TO THE MOST HIGH, AHAYAH!

Dear Family,

Once again, I hope you have enjoyed this segment of *My Time With The Most High*. I am especially happy to have the opportunity to present *Book Four* in this series because it represents the completion of the books of Moses. As we have learned, following the laws given to us by Our Power, Ahayah, is the first step toward reconnecting with our heritage, customs and culture. In addition to reclaiming our lost identity, the law also lays the foundation for the salvation of Israel and for Gentiles who are willing to follow the true path of Yashaya. Having said that, I pray you have really developed a love for the Law of The Most High!

The purpose of these workbooks is not to actually "teach" the Bible, but to offer a guide for self-study. It is my sincere prayer that all our young people will develop a love and passion for spending time with the Father through reading the Word, prayer and reflection/ meditation.

As this is not an actual textbook, there is no formal grading rubric. However, the writing assignments can be done verbally or used to spark discussion among a class or family unit. As mentioned, the target grade levels are fifth through eighth, but the writing assignments can be expanded for older students and shortened for the younger ones. Feel free to manipulate the prompts and activities to suit your needs. The main point is to get into the Word daily!

I must make a note about how the material was put together. All of the artwork and pictures came from online sources and are in no way products of my own talents. They are all available on public domain sites and are uncredited to any specific artist. Also, the puzzles were generated through TheTeachersCorner.net.

Shalom,

Sis Tara

Answer Key

Walking Into the Promises

Across

2- Jealous

3- Moses

6- Heathen

8- Aroer

9- Heshbon

10- Bashan

Down

1- Reuben and Gad

4- Exodus

5- Heart

6- Horeb

What's on the Menu

Across

2- Unclean

5- Divided

9- Abominable

10- Stranger

Down

1- Fins and Scales

3- Levite

4- Cud

6- Baldness

7- Peculiar

8- Three

Sweet 16

See if you can find the words hidden in the puzzle from Deuteronomy ch. 16 KJV.

```
M V Y Z X X N F A H S A C R I F I C E L
R U M J W D E S S E L B H N F Z T U B B
H K R U F Z I J N N T S N Q V Y W N G P
S C S X E K R L N Q U F H H U H D L P K
S K X Z B V V E V O R G G H N K Z E C N
W H A H T N E V E S V M I T A J Q A J J
D U N H M N D Q R H Y N C S M W P V E K
Q E L K C I S A T M B C N U D K X E S G
A P Y U P E C N A T I R E H N I U N O G
K F G S S E L R E H T A F T O A F E L U
O M D S B O P E I X T X B A B S R D E N
H G U T O N I Y L L S M E P N R E C M H
K A T R B Q G L S C I U W O C K M N N I
C D V A S P A P N N A B Z V P A E E S P
S P W N E L M S L O E N R D T W M U A Y
O T J G R K S Q W G S E R F J U B I B R
V P R E V O S S A P Z A E E M M E H I Z
T N Y R E J J M L F Y A E B B H R Q B U
V S S M I K I R H R S U L S L A X B P O
N Q E P W I D O W T J A D T A T T H K M
```

SACRIFICE	ABIB	SOLEMN
GROVE	INHERITANCE	TABERNACLE
UNLEAVENED	IMAGE	OBSERVE
REMEMBER	BONDMAN	SEASON
SEVENTH	FATHERLESS	SICKLE
WIDOW	STRANGER	FEAST
BLESSED	PASSOVER	

Ahayah Fights My Battles!!

1. Betrothed
2. Bulwarks
3. Besiege
4. Abominations
5. Tremble
6. Destroy
7. Battle
8. Chariots
9. Tributary
10. Officers

Un-Holy Abominations, Batman!

A. D14:10
B. D22:5
C. D18:10
D. D7:25
E. D15:23
F. D17:1
G. D14:3
H. D24:4
I. L20:13

Sabbath Day Law Quest

1. Lev. 23:11
2. Ex. 35:3
3. Lev. 24:8
4. Deut. 5:12
5. Lev. 26:2
6. Deut. 5:15

Blessed or Cursed?

Created with TheTeachersCorner.net Word Search Maker

Find the words below from the Book of Deuteronomy KJV.

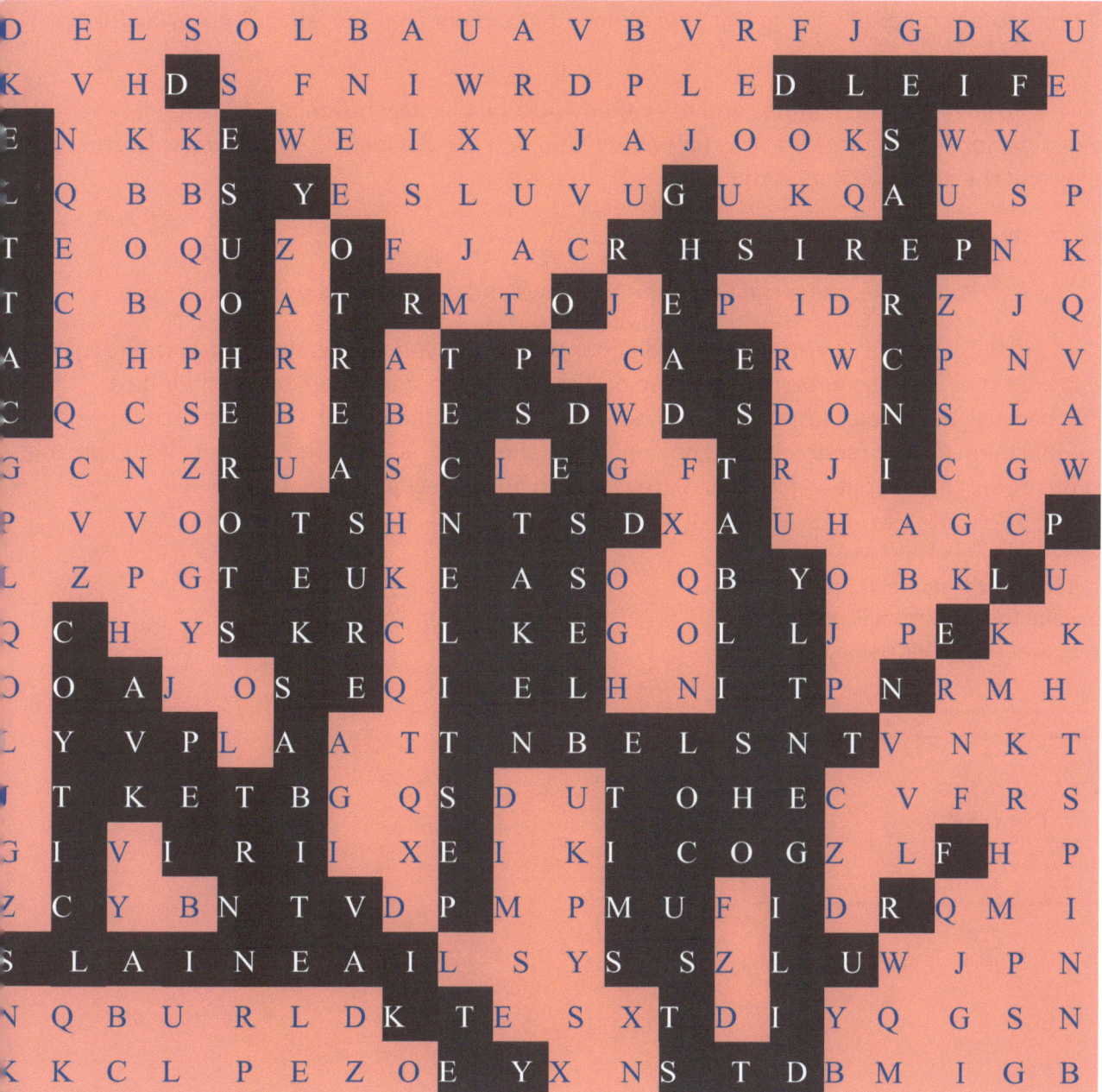

Appendix

Don't Be Led Astray- Divide group in half and give each group a sheet of paper and pencil. Set your timer to 3 minutes and have them brainstorm as many types of people who can lead others astray (preachers, teachers, friends, etc.). Tell them to be prepared with an example of how that person type can lead others away from Ahayah.

If students are more advanced, give 10 minutes and have them include a biblical reference **_or_** historical event that gives an example of a person leading others astray (ie Wives= Solomon's wives leading him to worship other gods, Prophets= Jim Jones and the poisoned Kool-Aid).

The team with the most verifiable person types and examples win.

All Ye, All Ye Outs In Free- Younger learners can find one-three laws and explain what each one means.

- **Make Flash Cards!** Cut several sheets of standard paper into eight even pieces. Have the learners write down one law on the front and write the scripture on the back. Encourage them to use their best handwriting because the whole class/ family will need to read what they write. Once the cards are completed, mix them up and randomly hold one up. If you show the passage, the student should be able to tell you the book, chapter and verse. This is great way to build precept knowledge as well.
- Example:

> Thou shalt not take the name of the LORD thy God in vain: for the LORD will not hold him guiltless that taketh his name in vain.

> Deut. 5:11